FIGHTING FORCES OF THE SECOND WORLD WAR

AT SEA

John C. Miles

W
FRANKLIN WATTS
LONDON·SYDNEY

First published in 2018
by Franklin Watts

Editor: Julia Bird
Series designer: John Christopher/White Design
Picture researcher: Diana Morris

ISBN 978 1 4451 5783 2

Printed in China

Franklin Watts
An imprint of
Hachette Children's Group
Part of The Watts Publishing Group
Carmelite House
50 Victoria Embankment
London EC4Y 0DZ

An Hachette UK company.
www.hachette.co.uk
www.franklinwatts.co.uk.

This book is dedicated to the memory of Vice-Admiral Sir Peter Berger RN (1925-2003),
who served on HMS *Ajax* during the Second World War.

Contents

War begins

In 1918 Germany lost the First World War and was forced to sign the Treaty of Versailles. Its harsh terms were very unpopular with Germans. In 1933 they elected a new leader, Adolf Hitler, who promised to make Germany great again.

Hitler rides through cheering crowds in the German city of Kassel in 1939.

Rise of the Nazis

Hitler's Nazi (National Socialist) Party believed that their country should rule over all others and that certain groups of people, such as Jews, were trying to cheat Germany. Under the Nazis, Germany began to build up its armed forces and take over land in nearby countries. Finally, on 1 September 1939 German forces invaded neighbouring Poland.

Allies and Axis powers

Britain and the countries of its empire and dominions, such as Canada and Australia, joined France to declare war on Germany. These countries became known as the Allies. During 1940 Hitler took control of Denmark, Norway, France, Belgium and the Netherlands. Italy joined the war on the side of the Nazis, forming the Axis forces. They were later bolstered by Japan. In June 1941 Germany invaded the Soviet Union. Then in December Japan attacked a US naval base, bringing the might of the USA into the war.

Nazi dictator Adolf Hitler, pictured in the late 1930s

4

The war turns

Throughout 1942 and 1943 Allied and Axis forces battled in North Africa, Italy, the Soviet Union and the Pacific as the war went global. Italy surrendered in September 1943. In June 1944, Allied forces launched Operation Overlord to begin taking back Europe. Months of fighting followed before the Allies began to advance towards Germany, something that the Soviet Union had begun to do from the east. Crushed in a massive pincer movement, Nazi forces were defeated. Hitler committed suicide at the end of April 1945 as Germany's capital, Berlin, fell to the Allies.

The atomic bomb

In the Pacific the war had raged on. To end it, US president Harry S. Truman authorised the use of the most terrible weapon ever invented – the atomic bomb – which obliterated the Japanese cities of Hiroshima and Nagasaki in August 1945. Japan finally surrendered. The Second World War was over.

The deadly atomic 'mushroom cloud' rises above Nagasaki.

A TERRIBLE TOLL

The cost of the war in human lives was staggering. Historians estimate that more than 21–25 million soldiers and up to 55 million civilians were killed. Around six million were Jews who were murdered by the Nazis during the Holocaust.

The Second World War at sea

Naval forces fought around the world during the Second World War, from the North Atlantic, where the Allies battled German submarines, to the South Pacific, where the US Navy and Australian and New Zealand forces fought the Imperial Japanese Navy. At the beginning of the war Britain's Royal Navy was the largest and most powerful in the world; by the end of the war the US Navy had expanded massively to become the world's biggest. This book looks at just some of the naval forces that fought during the war.

Torpedoed by a Nazi U-boat, a merchant ship sinks during the Battle of the Atlantic (see pages 6–7).

GERMAN U-BOATS

ACTIVE: 1939–45	STRENGTH: 1,140 vessels (1939–45)
AREAS ACTIVE: North Atlantic, North Sea, South Atlantic	

Within hours of the beginning of the Second World War in September 1939, Nazi U-boats (Unterseeboot or submarines) began attacking Allied ships, beginning the Battle of the Atlantic – the longest campaign of the Second World War.

Scapa Flow

U-boats were to prove Germany's most effective weapon in the war at sea, attacking Allied warships as well as merchant shipping (see pages 8–9). In October 1939 Captain Günther Prien managed to steer his submarine *U-47* undetected into the Royal Navy's base at Scapa Flow in Orkney off the north coast of Scotland. There he torpedoed and sank the British battleship HMS *Royal Oak*. This action shocked Britons, who had considered the base to be impregnable. Prien returned to a hero's welcome in Germany. Under Prien's command, *U-47* sank more than 30 Allied ships before it was in turn sunk in 1941.

U-boat Captain Günther Prien (directly below flag) and crew

HMS *Royal Oak*, which was sunk by *U-47*. More than 800 crew members died in the attack. The wreck of the ship lies under 30 m of water and is a protected war grave.

German shipyard workers launch a type VIIC U-boat in 1941.

TYPE VII U-BOAT

- **SPEED** 32 km/h on surface; 14 km/h submerged
- **RANGE** 15,700 km on surface; 150 km submerged

The type VII was the most common Nazi U-boat. It was armed with quick-firing 8.8-cm deck guns, plus anti-aircraft guns and up to 14 torpedoes. Carrying a crew of 44-52 officers and ratings, the type VII travelled on the surface most of the time, where its diesel engines powered it along at a speed of up to 32 km/h. When the ship submerged to attack the enemy or to escape an attack itself, the type VII used electric motors powered by batteries.

HMS Barham

In November 1941 the Royal Navy battleship HMS Barham was cruising off the coast of Egypt when it was intercepted by U-boat U-331. Hit by three torpedoes from a distance of only 375 m, Barham didn't stand a chance — a gigantic explosion blew the vessel apart, killing 862 men. The sinking (below) was captured by a news cameraman on board a nearby ship and remains a lasting record of the devastation wrought by a single U-boat attack.

From 1942 new anti-submarine weapons and tactics, plus the entry of the USA into the war, meant that the Allies were gradually able to win the battle against the German U-boats.

WHO'S WHO AT SEA IN THE SECOND WORLD WAR

Many types of warship fought at sea during the Second World War:

- Battleships and battlecruisers, armed with huge naval guns, were a navy's biggest ships. Below them were cruisers

- Aircraft carriers acted as floating airbases and allowed naval planes to strike at the enemy from the sea

- Fast-moving destroyers and corvettes had smaller guns, as well as torpedoes. They acted as escorts for bigger ships and played a key role in anti-submarine warfare

- Much smaller vessels such as landing craft delivered troops and tanks to a beach for a seaborne invasion.

Hit amidships, HMS Barham was ripped apart by a huge explosion. Amazingly, there were 487 survivors.

THE MERCHANT NAVY

	ACTIVE: 1939–45	STRENGTH: 185,000
	AREAS ACTIVE: Atlantic Ocean, Arctic Ocean	

Throughout the Battle of the Atlantic, the brave sailors of the Merchant Navy risked their lives to bring vital war supplies to Allied nations.

Essential service

As an island nation, Britain depended heavily on imports, needing more than one million tonnes of supplies per week just to allow it to survive and carry on the war. The only way to get this quantity of goods to Britain was by merchant ship. Nazi U-boat commanders were therefore ordered to sink as many Allied merchant ships as possible in a bid to cripple Britain's war effort.

Life on board

Life on merchant ships was hard, and food and accommodation for sailors was basic. Sailors 'signed on' for each voyage and did a variety of jobs, from ship-handling and navigation to shovelling coal into the ship's engines. The majority of seamen who crewed merchant ships were British. However there were also large numbers of sailors from India, China, the West Indies, Africa, Canada and Australia.

Crew members aboard the convoy escort destroyer HMS *Vanoc* watch over a nearby merchant ship.

Convoys

Merchant ships sailed together in large groups called convoys. Assembling in a harbour – such as Halifax on Canada's east coast – ships set off on their voyages escorted by smaller warships, such as destroyers and corvettes. These gave some protection from Nazi U-boats, but once enemy submarines located a convoy in the vastness of the ocean the results could be devastating – in September 1940 convoy HX72, consisting of 42 ships, was attacked by four U-boats. Over two days the convoy lost 11 of its ships.

TORPEDOED!

Many merchant ships were issued with light guns for self-defence but once torpedoed, a merchant ship had little chance of staying afloat. How quickly a ship sank depended on its cargo – if it was loaded with flammable aviation fuel there could be a huge explosion and few survivors. Ships carrying other goods sank more slowly, perhaps giving the crew time to launch lifeboats or swim to floating debris and await rescue by a nearby ship. Some U-boat crews even surfaced to pick up survivors. Nevertheless, thousands of sailors drowned in the freezing cold waters of the Atlantic.

Hit by a U-boat's torpedoes, an Allied merchant ship quickly sinks below the Atlantic waves.

ARCTIC CONVOYS

From 1941 to 1945 around 1,400 merchant ships formed 78 convoys that sailed from Britain, Iceland and North America to the Soviet Union, carrying key fighter planes, fuel, ammunition and food. Escorted by warships of the Royal Navy, Royal Canadian Navy and the US Navy, these convoys sailed around German-occupied Norway, braving U-boats, extreme seas and freezing Arctic weather conditions that left the ships coated in thick ice.

Crew members aboard HMS *Vansittart* hack away at more than 200 tonnes of ice while on Arctic convoy duty in February 1943.

CONVOY ESCORTS

	ACTIVE: 1940	STRENGTH: 294 ships
	AREAS ACTIVE: North Atlantic, Arctic	

Throughout the Second World War, small warships braved rough seas and deadly U-boat 'wolfpacks' to escort convoys safely across the Atlantic.

Tribal-class destroyer

These 115-m long all-purpose warships were developed in the 1930s, and used by the Royal Navy, the Royal Canadian Navy and the Royal Australian Navy. The ships were armed with eight 120-mm or 102-mm quick-firing naval guns and four 40-mm or 20-mm anti-aircraft guns, as well as torpedo tubes and 20 anti-submarine depth charges (see page 11). Able to speed along at 67 km/h and operated by a crew of 200, these warships were among the most modern used during the Second World War.

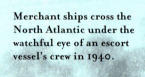

Merchant ships cross the North Atlantic under the watchful eye of an escort vessel's crew in 1940.

HMCS *HAIDA*

Only one Tribal-class destroyer – HMCS *Haida* – survives today, permanently moored in Hamilton, Ontario, Canada, as a museum ship. *Haida* and its sister ship, HMCS *Eskimo*, sank a German Type VII U-boat *U-971* in the English Channel on 24 June 1944.

Flower-class corvette

Below destroyers in size and firepower but far more numerous (267 were built), these light warships were mainly used as convoy protection vessels. They served with the Royal Navy, the Royal Canadian Navy and the US Navy, as well as the navies of Australia, New Zealand and other countries. Flower-class corvettes were 63 m long and carried a crew of 90. They were armed with a single 102-mm naval gun, three anti-aircraft guns, 70 depth charges (see below) and other anti-submarine weapons.

Anti-submarine weapons

Once a U-boat was detected, naval commanders attacked it with a range of weapons. Depth charges were underwater bombs set to explode at a certain depth – if one blew up near a U-boat the underwater shock wave could split the submarine's hull, allowing water to rush in and sink it. 'Hedgehog' or 'Squid' anti-submarine bombs were fired over the bow of an attacking ship. These weapons had contact fuses so that they had to hit the submarine in order to explode, but were much more effective than depth charges.

Royal Navy crew load a depth charge into a thrower.

ASDIC AND SONAR

Initially developed during the First World War, ASDIC (Anti-Submarine Detection) and SONAR (Sound Navigation And Ranging) worked by transmitting underwater pulses of sound. These bounced off an object – such as a submarine – and returned to the transmitter, sometimes as a 'ping' sound in the operator's headphones. The louder and more frequent the pings were, the closer the object. Based on this information a decision could be made to launch an attack. Navies also used hydrophones, or underwater microphones, to listen for the sound of a submarine's propellers.

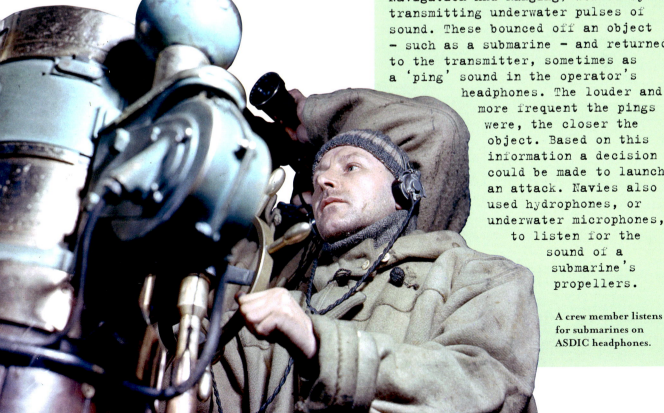

A crew member listens for submarines on ASDIC headphones.

BATTLESHIP *BISMARCK*

	LAUNCHED: 1939	CREW STRENGTH: 2,200
	AREAS ACTIVE: North Sea, North Atlantic	

In 1941 a tense game of cat and mouse was played out in the North Atlantic, as the Royal Navy tried to locate and destroy one of Nazi Germany's most powerful warships.

The *Bismarck*

Launched in 1939, the battleship *Bismarck* was a 251-m-long floating fortress. It was armed with eight huge 38-cm naval guns in four swivelling armoured turrets, 44 smaller naval guns and anti-aircraft guns. German naval commanders intended to use the *Bismarck* to attack Allied merchant shipping in the North Atlantic. In 1941, *Bismarck* was moved to Nazi-occupied Norway for safety and anchored in a fjord (narrow sea inlet) with the cruiser *Prinz Eugen* and escorting destroyers.

The Royal Navy battlecruiser HMS *Hood*

Battle of the Denmark Strait

On 21 May 1941, *Bismarck* and *Prinz Eugen* left Norway and headed for the Atlantic. They were shadowed by a Royal Navy squadron including the battlecruiser HMS *Hood*. On 24 May the two sides met in battle in the Denmark Strait, but after only ten minutes one of *Bismarck*'s massive shells hit the *Hood* amidships, exploding its main magazine. The *Hood* broke in two and sank in just three minutes, killing 1,415 men.

The *Bismarck* pictured firing its main battery of eight 38-cm guns.

Find the *Bismarck*!

The *Bismarck* had been damaged in the battle so Admiral Günther Lütjens decided to head for the port of St Nazaire in Nazi-occupied France, where repairs could be made. But the Royal Navy had other ideas and sent a massive task force to sink it.

A first attack by torpedo bomber planes scored one hit, but the *Bismarck* then managed to slip away. Eventually, however, British code-breakers deciphered messages sent by the enemy. This, combined with the use of onboard radar (see box right), allowed the Royal Navy to work out the *Bismarck*'s new position. A new wave of torpedo planes from HMS *Ark Royal* then moved in; one torpedo scored a direct hit on *Bismarck*'s port rudder, leaving the ship unable to steer as the British task force approached.

A British Fairey Swordfish bomber launches a torpedo.

Sinking

At daybreak on 27 May the business of sinking the *Bismarck* began, as shell after shell from battleships HMS *Rodney* and HMS *King George V* pounded the enemy. The *Bismarck* could not return fire accurately but its remaining crew refused to surrender. By 10 am the *Bismarck* was a smoking wreck but still afloat, protected by its thick hull armour. Eventually the *Bismarck*'s crew set off demolition charges to sink what remained of the ship as HMS *Dorsetshire* launched a torpedo attack. The *Bismarck* sank at 10.40 am; out of its crew of 2,200 there were only 114 survivors.

RADAR

This technology was developed in great secrecy during the 1930s, and played a key part in the Second World War. Radar stands for 'Radio Detection And Ranging'. In radar systems, a transmitter sends out pulses of radio waves, which bounce off an object such as a ship before returning to the system's receiver. The operator can then work out how far away the object is and how fast it is travelling. Radar was key to Britain's victory in the Battle of Britain and was also used extensively in the war at sea.

Radar operators helped direct the ship's gunfire at the enemy.

ARMOUR ON SHIPS

Warships were protected by hardened steel armour up to 360 mm thick. Armour was thickest on a ship's hull, gun turrets and on the 'citadel', which included the bridge from where the ship was commanded and steered. Most ships had thinner armour on their decks to save weight. As the loss of HMS *Hood* demonstrated, in the event of a direct hit this could be a critical weak spot.

FREE FRENCH NAVAL FORCES

FORMED:
1940

AREAS ACTIVE:
Western Europe, Pacific

STRENGTH:
1 obsolete aircraft carrier, 2 battleships, 2 cruisers, 5 destroyers, 22 escort vessels, 9 submarines, numerous other small vessels

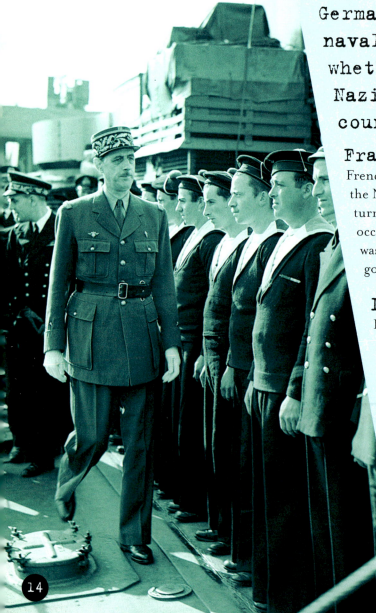

When France was invaded by Germany in June 1940, French naval forces had to choose whether to go along with the Nazi occupation of their country or to help fight it.

France splits

French leader Philippe Pétain signed an armistice with the Nazis on 22 June. This ended the fighting, but turned the northern part of France into a German occupation zone. The southern part of the country was controlled by a French government – the 'Vichy' government – which was sympathetic to the Nazis.

De Gaulle's appeal

French General Charles de Gaulle, who had escaped to London, made a famous radio speech in which he appealed to the French military and civilians everywhere to join his 'Free French Forces' and continue the war by fighting with the Allies. Days after de Gaulle made this appeal, Admiral Émile Muselier joined de Gaulle; the crew of the submarine *Narval* also pledged support. This, plus the acquisition of the few ships – such as the destroyer *Léopard* – that had been docked in British ports, meant that the Free French possessed the beginnings of a naval force.

General de Gaulle, leader of the Free French forces, inspects officers and sailors on board the destroyer *Léopard*.

The navy grows

As the war progressed, the Free French fleet grew in size. It received a big boost in November 1942 when the territory of French West Africa, which had previously supported the Vichy regime, declared its support for de Gaulle. As a result, the Free French navy acquired a modern battleship, the *Richelieu*, one heavy and three light cruisers plus several destroyers, all of which had been stationed at the port of Dakar.

The heavy cruiser *Montcalm* had been stationed in Dakar.

JACQUES COUSTEAU

One of the most well-known members of the Free French naval forces was the diver and film-maker Jacques Cousteau (1910-1997). He co-developed the aqua-lung in the mid-1940s and took part in many commando operations during the war.

In action

During the D-Day landings on 6 June 1944 (see pages 24–25), 11 Free French ships took part in Operation Neptune, the naval action that supported Allied invasion forces. Heavy ships such as the cruiser *Montcalm* bombarded the Nazis with gunfire as troops swept ashore on the beaches of Normandy. Free French naval commandos also attacked German positions on the cliffs above the invasion beaches.

Some Free French ships, such as the destroyer *Triomphant*, served in the Pacific area, where its crew helped to evacuate civilians ahead of the invasion of Nauru in 1942. Later the ship helped to protect Australia from Japanese attack.

A battleship pounds Nazi defences on D-Day, while landing craft prepare to deliver troops onto the beaches of Normandy.

ITALIAN REGIA MARINA & THE 10ᵀᴴ ASSAULT FLOTILLA

FORMED:	STRENGTH:
1940	200 vessels
AREAS ACTIVE: Mediterranean	

Italy joined the Second World War on the Axis side after the fall of France. In the Mediterranean, the Italian navy posed a very real threat to the might of Britain's Royal Navy.

The Regia Marina

At the beginning of the war the Italian navy, or Regia Marina, looked like a formidable force. It had six battleships, 19 cruisers, 59 destroyers and other vessels including torpedo boats and submarines. However, many Italian vessels were obsolete, lacking modern equipment such as radar. There were operational issues as well. In battle, Regia Marina commanders were required to seek approval from their bosses on shore before taking critical action. This often resulted in a missed opportunity to deal a decisive blow to the enemy.

War in the Mediterranean

During the early part of the war, the Royal Navy and the Regia Marina battled for control of the Mediterranean Sea. The Royal Navy's bases in Gibraltar, Malta and Egypt were key to its ability to protect the Suez Canal and the sea route to British India — making them high-priority Axis targets.

Many Italian naval vessels, like this submarine, were out of date and unable to tackle the more modern equipment of the Royal Navy.

10th Assault Flotilla

This elite Italian naval special forces unit was created in 1940, shortly after Italy entered the war. By the end of the war the unit had sunk more than 72,000 tonnes of Allied warships and more than 130,000 tonnes of merchant shipping. The 10th Flotilla used a range of innovative methods to attack Allied ships, including MT assault boats (see box right) and SLC torpedoes (bottom).

An MT assault boat

MT ASSAULT BOATS

- **CREW** 1
- **EXPLOSIVE CHARGE** 300 kg

These were small fast motorboats, each of which was packed with 300 kg of explosives. Launched from a destroyer, the assault boat's operator would speed towards the target, then jump overboard before impact. On 25 March 1941 an MT squadron attacked British ships at Suda Bay on the island of Crete. The heavy cruiser HMS *York* was heavily damaged. The commandos also sank two oil tankers and a cargo ship.

SLC TORPEDOS

- **CREW** 2
- **EXPLOSIVE CHARGE** 300 kg

The most famous weapon used by the 10th Flotilla was the SLC manned torpedo, nicknamed the *Maiale*, or 'pig'. On 3 December 1941 the Italian submarine *Sciré* delivered three *Maiale* to the harbour at Alexandria, Egypt, where the Royal Navy battleships HMS *Valiant* and *Queen Elizabeth* were at anchor. The mines they placed sank the two British battleships, as well as a Norwegian tanker. The battleships sank in only a few metres of water and were later refloated and repaired, but the attack put them out of action for more than a year.

HMS *Queen Elizabeth* (centre), and (right) two frogmen ride an SLC manned torpedo through a battleship's anti-torpedo nets.

ROYAL MARINE COMMANDOS

FORMED: 1940	STRENGTH 6,000–8,000
AREAS ACTIVE: Western Europe, Asia	

Founded in 1940 and active throughout the Second World War, Royal Marine Commando units became famous for carrying out daring seaborne raids in enemy territory.

Origins

The Royal Marines were historically soldiers who fought with the Royal Navy. Founded by Prime Minister Winston Churchill, the first 'Special Service Brigades' – later known as Commandos – included personnel from both the British Army and Royal Marines. Each Commando battalion contained about 450 men, organised into troops of 75 and sub-sections of 15. By 1942 6,000 Royal Marines had volunteered for Commando units, and by the end of the war nine RM Commando battalions had been raised.

Commandos smile for the camera as they return from a daring mission to capture Nazi radar equipment in June 1942.

Tough training

By 1942 Commando recruits trained in Scotland where, on arrival, they had to perform a 13-km march from the railway station to their training camp while carrying all their equipment. Training focused on extreme physical fitness, and those who failed to make the grade were marked 'RTU' or 'return to unit'. Commando training exercises used live ammunition and explosives to make conditions as real as possible, and the skills recruits learned included survival, river crossings, mountain climbing and hand-to-hand fighting techniques.

Operations

RM Commando units conducted a range of daring operations against enemy forces during the course of the Second World War. In 1940 and 1941 Commandos supported Allied campaigns against German forces in occupied Norway, spearheading attacks on enemy positions and factories producing war supplies. In 1942 and 1943 Commando units took part in the landings in North Africa, Sicily and Italy, and on 6 June 1944 Commandos went ashore on D-Day (see pages 24–25). Towards the end of the war, Commando units fought bravely against Japanese forces in Burma (now Myanmar).

Commandos in training, 1942

COCKLESHELL HEROES

In December 1942 ten RM Commandos attacked ships carrying enemy war supplies in the harbour at Bordeaux, France. The men set off from a submarine in five two-man folding canoes known as Cockles. Two men were drowned when their craft capsized; another four were captured and shot by the Germans.

The remaining four Commandos eventually reached Bordeaux harbour by paddling under cover of darkness. They attached mines to the hulls of six ships which exploded and caused severe damage. After the operation was complete, two more of the cockleshell heroes were captured and shot, while the final two escaped to safety in neutral Spain.

Two Commando raiders pictured with their 'cockleshell' canoe.

THE IMPERIAL JAPANESE NAVY

	ACTIVE: 1941-45	**STRENGTH (1941):** 10 battleships, 10 aircraft carriers, 38 cruisers, 112 destroyers, 65 submarines, support vessels
	AREAS ACTIVE: Pacific	

The government that controlled Japan in the 1930s attempted to dominate the Pacific region, invading China in 1937 and attacking the USA in 1941 (see pages 26-27). As an island nation, the might of the Imperial Japanese Navy (IJN) was key to the country's early military successes in the Second World War.

Preparing for war

Since the 1870s, Japan had been building up and modernising its navy. As early as 1920 the Imperial Japanese Navy was the third biggest in the world, after Britain and the USA. By the late 1930s, Japan had scored several important naval firsts. It had launched the world's first purpose-built aircraft carrier, the *Hōshō*, in 1921, had pioneered the use of very large guns on battleships and had developed modern destroyers armed with advanced torpedoes. But the IJN lagged behind other nations in submarine warfare, technology such as radar and secure communications.

The IJN aircraft carrier *Hōshō*

Aircraft aboard an IJN aircraft carrier prepare to attack Pearl Harbor on 7 December 1941 (see page 26).

Early success and defeat

Throughout 1941 and 1942 the armed forces of Japan steamrollered through the Pacific region, inflicting heavy defeats on the Allies. On 10 December 1941 Japanese naval aircraft sank two Royal Navy battleships, HMS *Repulse* and HMS *Prince of Wales* in the South China Sea. In April 1942, the IJN attacked the Royal Navy in the Indian Ocean, making part of the force retreat to East Africa.

The Japanese navy's seemingly unstoppable advance was eventually checked by a series of devastating defeats at the hands of the Allies, beginning at the Battle of Midway in June 1942. By 1943 the Allies, particularly the USA, were able to build new ships and replace battle losses much faster than Japan, which was beginning to run short of war materials and combat-trained personnel.

```
----------------------------------

YAMATO
----------------------------------

• SPEED 50 km/h
• RANGE Range 13,300 km

This monster ship and its sister
ship, the Mushashi, were the biggest
battleships ever constructed.
Launched in 1940, the Yamato was 263
m long and was armed with nine huge
46-cm naval guns, 12 15.5-cm guns,
12 127-mm guns and 28 anti-aircraft
guns. It carried seven aircraft and
had steel armour that was 650 mm
thick in places. In April 1945, as
the Allies battled with the Japanese
for the island of Okinawa, Yamato
was sent as part of a counter-attack
force but was instead attacked
by wave after wave of Allied air
strikes. After 11 torpedo hits and
more than six direct bomb hits, the
huge ship rolled over, blew up and
sank, killing an estimated 3,055
crew members.
```

The battleship *Yamato* nears completion in a Japanese dockyard

THE SPECIAL BOAT SECTION

FORMED:	STRENGTH:
1940	100-250 approx
AREAS ACTIVE:	
Mediterranean, Asia	

Like the Royal Marine Commandos, the Special Boat Section was founded in 1940 to conduct dangerous secret missions. Renamed the Special Boat Service after the war, today the unit is still part of the UK's Special Forces.

Eccentric founder

The Special Boat Section was founded by Roger Courtney, a Commando. Courtney was convinced that a small naval force, operating from folding kayaks, could boost the war effort by conducting raids on enemy shipping. Courtney's first attempts to convince Royal Navy officials of the worth of his idea were unsuccessful. So, while in Scotland, Courtney paddled to a British warship, HMS *Glengyle*, anchored in the River Clyde. There he secretly climbed aboard and wrote his initials on the door to the captain's cabin before stealing a deck gun cover. Afterwards Courtney went to a nearby hotel where a group of high-ranking Royal Navy officers were meeting and presented them with the cover. He was promoted to Captain and given command of a new unit, the Special Boat Section.

A corporal of the SBS prepares his weapons for action.

Mediterranean ops

The men of the SBS deployed to the Mediterranean in 1941, working with the 1st Submarine Flotilla – the vessels of which delivered SBS men to their targets. The SBS undertook reconnaissance missions on enemy-occupied Greek islands and supported the evacuation of troops from Crete. A second unit, No 2 SBS, was formed in December 1941.

Greek boats of the type that transported SBS members to their targets. The vessels were typically armed with one 50-mm cannon and two machine guns.

Airfield raids

In June 1942 No 1 SBS raided airfields on German-occupied Crete and, in September, Rhodes, which were being used by enemy aircraft to attack British convoys in the Mediterranean. In the Rhodes operation, codenamed 'Operation Anglo', the SBS managed to destroy numerous aircraft, a fuel dump and some buildings, but only two men returned to the waiting submarine – the rest were captured and became prisoners of war.

Later missions

After these operations No 1 SBS became part of the Special Air Service (SAS) and was renamed the Special Boat Squadron. They worked with Greek special forces and, in 1944, fought alongside the Allies in Greece and Italy. No 2 SBS did vital reconnaissance work for US forces in North Africa in November 1942, then supported Allied landings in Sicily, before being redeployed to the campaign against Japanese forces in Burma towards the end of the war.

MAJOR ANDERS LASSEN

One of the most famous SBS officers, Lassen was born in Copenhagen and arrived in Britain shortly after the beginning of the war. He trained as a Commando, then became a member of the SBS, rising to the rank of major by 1944. Lassen served in the Mediterranean, North Africa, Greece, north-west Europe, the Balkans and Italy. Having won three Military Crosses for his brave actions in a series of daring operations, Lassen was killed in April 1945 while leading a raid on a German position in Italy. After his death he was awarded the Victoria Cross, Britain's highest bravery award.

US NAVY COMBAT DEMOLITION TEAMS

FORMED: 1942–43	STRENGTH: 3,500
AREAS ACTIVE: Western Europe, Pacific	

On 6 June 1944 the Allies launched D-Day – the biggest seaborne invasion in history. The US Navy's specialist naval demolition teams cleared pathways under heavy fire so Allied tanks could go ashore.

Beginnings

The combat demolition teams had their early origins in the costly Allied landings at Gallipoli during the First World War, where thousands of British and ANZAC troops were pinned down and slaughtered by enemy fire. US military leaders later studied the landings and began to develop new techniques for amphibious warfare by the mid-1930s.

Operation Torch

For Operation Torch – the Allied landings in North Africa in November 1942 – the US Navy employed demolition units as part of its special forces. The six-man teams landed ahead of the main US forces, clearing obstacles such as cables and defensive nets. After this success, US Navy commanders created a specialist force to take on these tasks – the Naval Combat Demolition Units.

(Left) Members of a NCDU, having completed their mission, watch Japanese attacks on 1 July 1945 and (inset) an NCDU combat swimmer in action.

Training for D-Day

By early 1944 thousands of Allied troops were stationed in Britain, training for D-Day in June. These included 34 NCDU assault teams, each containing 13 men. The scale of the upcoming task was immense – the beaches where the landings were to take place were heavily defended by the Nazis, who had built elaborate obstacles to stop any attempts to stage landings. On some beaches three-tonne steel barricades called 'Belgian gates' had been placed in the surf, while just inland were mines, fortified machine guns and mortar positions.

Going ashore

At daybreak on 6 June 1944 D-Day began, and US forces landed on Omaha and Utah beaches. The NCDUs went ashore with the second wave of landings in order to clear 15-m gaps in the beach defences so that tanks and other vehicles could get onto the beach. Under heavy fire the teams began to plant their explosives and clear obstacles. By the end of the day 13 gaps had been cleared on Omaha beach, at a cost of 31 men killed and 60 wounded.

IN THE PACIFIC

The Pacific US Navy demolition units were called Underwater Demolition Teams, or UDTs. They were formed in response to the Battle of Tarawa in November 1943, where faulty reconnaissance nearly caused a landing by US Marines to fail. UDTs were active in all the major US actions during the Pacific campaign, including Luzon, Guam, Iwo Jima, Leyte and Okinawa. In this latter action nearly 1,000 UDT members provided reconnaissance and demolition support for the invasion.

At Utah Beach, 16 pathways were cleared with four killed and 11 wounded. The brave actions of the NCDUs ensured that weapons and reinforcements could keep pouring onto the beaches to allow troops to fight their way inland.

US troops wade ashore on Omaha Beach on D-Day. The work of US NCDUs helped to make the landings possible.

THE US PACIFIC FLEET

COMMANDER UNITED STATES PACIFIC FLEET	**ACTIVE:** 1941–45	**STRENGTH:** (1941) 3 aircraft carriers, 9 battleships, 24 cruisers, 80 destroyers, 56 submarines.
	AREAS ACTIVE: Pacific	(1945) 27 aircraft carriers, 8 battleships and more than 1,150 other vessels

Naval forces were **vital** to the Allied war effort in the Pacific Ocean. The US Navy's Pacific Fleet bore the brunt of much of the fighting. Here are three critical naval actions fought in the Pacific.

Pearl Harbor

On 7 December 1941 Japanese forces attacked the US naval and air base at Pearl Harbor, Hawaii. Waves of carrier-based planes from the Imperial Japanese First Air Fleet launched a surprise attack at 7.48 am. By the end of the day six US ships – including four battleships – had been sunk, 13 ships damaged and 188 planes destroyed. More than 2,400 US personnel were killed in the attack. The USA declared war on Japan the next day.

The attack on Pearl Harbor, as seen from a Japanese aircraft. US ships lie at anchor in the foreground.

Battle of Midway

This decisive naval battle took place on 4–7 June 1942, when Japanese forces again attempted to wipe out the US Pacific Fleet. Japanese commanders had planned to ambush US ships near the island of Midway but didn't realise that their secret messages had been intercepted by US code-breakers. This allowed the Americans to stage their own ambush. Seven aircraft carriers were involved in this battle – three American and four Japanese. All four Japanese carriers, plus one heavy cruiser, were sunk. The US lost one carrier, the USS *Yorktown*, and one destroyer.

The Japanese cruiser *Mikuma* sinks at the Battle of Midway.

Battle of Leyte Gulf

This epic encounter, believed by many to be the biggest naval battle in history, took place in the Philippines from 23–26 October 1944. In an attempt to starve Japan of vital oil supplies, US forces invaded the island of Leyte on 20 October. To oppose them, Japanese commanders sent in almost all their remaining navy, including nine battleships and four aircraft carriers. Allied forces included 16 aircraft carriers and 12 battleships. The battle ended in a crushing defeat for Japan, which lost four aircraft carriers, three battleships, 10 cruisers and more than 12,500 men. The Imperial Japanese Navy never sailed again as a large force.

US Navy ships used smokescreens, as shown here, to deter Japanese air attacks during the Battle of Leyte Gulf in 1944.

ANZAC SQUADRON

This squadron, containing ships of the Australian, New Zealand and US navies, was formed in February 1942 to defend northeastern Australia from Japan. The flagship, HMAS *Australia* (above), was armed with eight-200 mm guns, six anti-aircraft guns and eight torpedo tubes, had a crew of more than 800 and could sail at 57 km/h.

X-CLASS MIDGET SUBMARINES

FORMED:
1943

STRENGTH:
100 personnel approx

AREAS ACTIVE:
Western Europe, Asia

Many nations used stealthy midget submarines during the war at sea. One of the most famous was the British X-craft.

A Royal Navy midget submarine on trial in a Scottish loch in 1940.

Mini raiders

Midget submarines were developed to carry out stealth missions, such as entering an enemy harbour in order to damage shipping or communications. The vessels were roughly a quarter the length of a normal submarine and carried between one and six crew members. They were designed to be towed to their operating area by a full-sized submarine and towed back to base after the mission was complete.

The cramped interior of an X-craft.

X-craft

These famous midget submarines were built for the Royal Navy from 1943. Crewed by three men – commander, pilot and engineer – the subs were only 15.6 m long. They were powered by a 42 hp four-cylinder diesel engine for running on the surface and an electric motor for travelling while submerged.

The X-craft's normal armament was two high-explosive charges carried on either side of the vessel. In an attack, the crew would drop these underneath the target and set time fuses to go off.

Operation Source

In September 1943 the Royal Navy launched a daring raid code-named Operation Source. Here, X-craft attacked Nazi warships – one of which was the *Bismarck*'s sister battleship *Tirpitz* – which were anchored in a Norwegian fjord. The raid was beset by problems – two of the six X-craft were lost at sea on the journey north and two more never made it to their targets – but *X6* and *X7* managed to place their charges, which went off. This caused considerable damage to *Tirpitz* and kept the ship out of action for months. After the mission, unable to escape, the crews of *X6* and *X7* had to abandon their subs. All were captured and made prisoners of war.

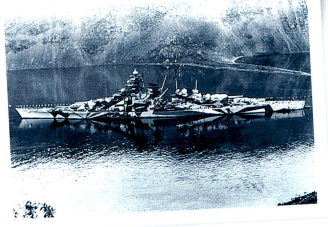
The Nazi battleship *Tirpitz*, shown here, was attacked by X-craft in 1943.

Operation Postage Able

Early in 1944 *X20* undertook a dangerous three-day mission, gathering key information about the Normandy coastline right under the noses of its Nazi defenders. The crew carried out depth soundings and reconnaissance by day and landed divers ashore at night to collect soil samples. This information helped Allied commanders plan the pivotal D-Day landings.

Towards the end of the war, in the Far East, the four-man XE craft was deployed in operations against Japanese forces.

Glossary

Aircraft carrier A warship used as a floating airbase.

Allied powers The military forces of Britain and its empire and dominions, France, the USA and, after 1941, Russia.

amidships In the middle of a ship.

amphibious An attack from the sea that delivers troops and tanks, etc. onto a beach.

armament Weapons and military equipment.

armistice An agreement between warring sides to stop fighting.

artillery Guns bigger than machine guns and rifles.

Axis The military forces of Nazi Germany, Italy, Japan and some other countries.

battlecruiser A large warship with some big guns, which is between a cruiser and a battleship in size.

battleship A huge warship.

bow The front of a ship.

bridge The part of a large ship from where it is steered and commanded.

capsize When a ship rolls over in the water, usually before sinking.

code-breaker Someone who works out what an enemy's coded messages mean.

Commando Elite special operations troops who are trained to perform dangerous secret missions.

convoy A large fleet of ships travelling together for protection.

corvette A small, fast warship.

cruiser A medium-sized warship armed with some heavy guns.

demolition Blowing up military targets with explosives.

deploy To send into action.

depth charge An underwater bomb that explodes at a certain depth.

destroyer A small, fast warship armed with light guns.

dictator A leader who wields supreme power to control a country and its people.

Fascist A political movement of the 1930s where a country unites as a disciplined force behind a nationalistic, all-powerful leader.

fuse A device that makes a larger bomb or torpedo explode; a detonator.

Holocaust The organised murder of Jews, Roma (gypsies) and gay people by the Nazis during the Second World War.

hull The main body of a ship.

impregnable Unable to be successfully attacked.

intercept To catch up with a target in order to attack it.

landing craft A flat-bottomed craft designed to deliver soldiers and vehicles onto a beach.

magazine The part of a warship where ammunition and explosives are stored.

manoeuvre To move in a certain way.

Merchant Navy A fleet of ships that goes to sea to carry on trade in goods rather than war.

1939

1 September Nazi Germany invades Poland; the Second World War begins

3 September Britain and France declare war on Germany

September British Expeditionary Force (BEF) sails for France

September Battle of the Atlantic begins; German U-boats sink Allied merchant shipping in the Atlantic Ocean

October HMS Royal Oak sunk by a German U-boat at its base in Orkney

1940

April/May Nazi Germany invades Denmark and Norway

10 May Nazi Germany invades the Netherlands, Belgium and France

26 May Operation Dynamo – the Allied evacuation at Dunkirk, begins. Royal Navy and civilian ships play a big part in the evacuation

11 June Italy joins the war on the Axis side

10 July-31 October The Battle of Britain – Britain's Royal Air Force defeats Nazi Luftwaffe

September 1940– May 1941 Nazi 'Blitz' (aerial bombing campaign) on Britain

1941

February Hitler sends Rommel's Afrika Korps to North Africa

April Italy and Germany attack Yugoslavia, Greece and Crete

24 May Nazi battleship *Bismarck* sinks HMS *Hood*

24-27 May *Bismarck* is hunted down and sunk by the Royal Navy

22 June Nazis invade Soviet Russia

July Nazi naval 'Enigma' code cracked by Allied code-breakers

7 December Japanese attack the US Navy at Pearl Harbor; USA enters war on Allied side

December Italian forces attack Royal Navy ships with manned torpedoes

nationalist Someone who believes their country is better than others.

navigation Finding the way at sea.

Nazi A member of Adolf Hitler's National Socialist Workers' Party or, in the context of this book, a member of the German armed forces during the Second World War.

neutral A country that doesn't take sides in a war and refuses to fight.

obliterate To destroy or wipe out utterly.

obsolete A machine that is old and not effective any more.

offensive A planned military attack.

pincer movement A military strategy designed to encircle and trap enemy forces.

prisoner of war A soldier taken captive and held by enemy forces during a war.

ratings Members of a navy.

reconnaissance Finding out information about an enemy's strength by observing or photographing its positions.

stern The back of a ship.

torpedo An underwater missile dropped from a plane or fired from a submarine in order to sink an enemy ship.

U-boat A German submarine; short for *Unterseeboot*.

war crime A crime against humanity, for example, deliberately killing unarmed prisoners or civilians during a war.

Find out more

Books

Moments in History (Wayland, 2015)
True Stories: World War Two, Clive Gifford (Wayland, 2013)
World War Two (Franklin Watts, 2015)

Websites

www.bbc.co.uk/history/worldwars/wwtwo
The BBC's history site on the Second World War.

www.iwm.org.uk/history/second-world-war
The Second World War section of the Imperial War Museum's website.

www.nmrn.org.uk
The website of the National Museum of the Royal Navy.

www.submarine-museum.co.uk
The website of the Royal Navy Submarine Museum.

www.warmuseum.ca
The Canadian War Museum's website.

https://www.awm.gov.au
The website of the Australian War Memorial.

http://www.nationalww2museum.org
The website of the National World War Two Museum

Note to parents and teachers: Every effort has been made by the Publishers to ensure that the websites in this book are suitable for children, that they are of highest educational value and that they contain no inappropriate or offensive material. However, because of the nature of the Internet, it is impossible to guarantee that contents of these sites will not be altered. We strongly advise that Internet access is supervised by a responsible adult.

1942

15 February Japanese capture Singapore and take 60,000 Allied prisoners

February ANZAC squadron formed

May Battle of Bir Hakeim

4-7 June US Navy defeats Japanese at key Battle of Midway

June SBS raids airfields in Crete

11 November Allies defeat Afrika Korps at El Alamein

November Battle of Stalingrad begins

8 November Operation Torch begins – US troops land in North Africa; US NCDUs help clear beaches

1943

2 February Soviet forces defeat Nazi forces at Stalingrad

13 May Axis forces surrender in North Africa; 275,000 taken prisoner

9 July Allies invade Sicily

July-August Battle of Kursk

3 September Allied forces invade Italy at Salerno; RM Commandos take part in the landings

8 September Italy surrenders; Nazi Germany now opposes Allied advance through Italy

September Royal Navy X-craft attack German battleship *Tirpitz*

1944

22 January Allied forces land at Anzio, Italy

January-May Key battle of Monte Cassino in Italy

5 June Rome liberated

6 June D-Day – Allied armies invade Normandy to begin freeing Europe from Nazi forces. RM Commandos and US NCDUs, as well as ships of the Royal Navy, US Navy and the Free French Navy play key roles

25 August Paris liberated

23-26 October Key naval battle of Leyte Gulf in the Pacific wipes out much of the IJN

16 December Battle of the Bulge begins – Nazi Germany launches its final, unsuccessful offensive in the Ardennes region of France

1945

23 March Allied forces cross the River Rhine into Germany

April/May Soviet forces close in on Berlin; Hitler kills himself on 30 April as the German capital falls

7 May Nazi forces surrender

8 May VE (Victory in Europe) Day – the war in Europe ends

6 August, 9 August US drops atomic bombs on Hiroshima and Nagasaki

15 August Japan surrenders; VJ (Victory over Japan) Day – the war in the Far East ends

Index

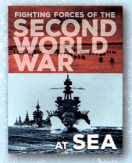

978 1 4451 5783 2

AT SEA

- War begins
- U-boats
- The Merchant Navy
- *Bismarck*
- The Free French Naval Forces
- The Italian 10th Light Flotilla
- Royal Marine Commandos
- Allied Convoy Escorts
- The Japanese Naval Forces
- The Special Boat Service
- US NCDUs
- The US Pacific Fleet
- X-craft

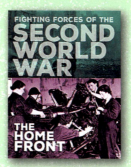

978 1 4451 5787 0

THE HOME FRONT

- War begins
- Polish fighters
- The French Resistance
- The Home Guard
- ARP and Fire Services
- Female defenders of the Soviet Union
- The Home Front in the USA
- The Special Operations Executive
- The German Civil Defence
- Code-breakers
- Partisans
- Women at war
- The battle for Berlin

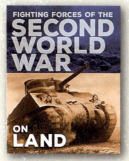

978 1 4451 5746 7

ON LAND

- War begins
- The British Expeditionary Force
- The Afrika Korps
- The French Foreign Legion
- The Long Range Desert Group
- The 7TH Australian Infantry Division
- The Special Air Service
- USSR 6ND Army
- Waffen-SS Panzer Divisions
- 1ST Special Service Force
- US 1ST Infantry Division
- US Rangers
- The Chindits

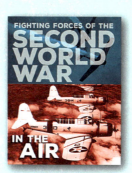

978 1 4451 5785 6

IN THE AIR

- War begins
- The Luftwaffe
- RAF Fighter Command
- Luftwaffe Fallschirmjäger
- The Imperial Navy 1st Air Fleet
- Doolittle's Raiders
- Bomber Command
- The Air Transport Auxiliary
- RAF 617 Squadron 'Dambusters'
- Sturmovik Ground Attack Squadrons
- Allied Airborne Divisions
- Kamikaze Squadrons
- 509TH Composite Group